CW00404170

THE VISION SINGS

SINGS

John Arlott
The Voice of Cricket

Editor: Richard Jones
Design: Joe Burt
Production Editor: Anne Smith

ISBN: 0-9553520-6-1
The first moral right of the author has been asserted.

First published in Great Britain in 2007 by Toilet Books,
3 Monmouth Place, Bath BA1 2AT.

Toilet Books is an imprint of Naked Guides Ltd, (trading as Tangent Books).

Pictures supplied by Empics

Thanks to Tim Arlott.

Collected by **Alex Murphy**

This book is dedicated to the memory of Leslie Thomas John Arlott. Born February 25, 1914, in Basingstoke, Hants. Died December 14, 1991, on Alderney, Channel Islands.

" You're not only the best cricket commentator – far and away that; but the best sports commentator I've heard, ever; exact, enthusiastic, prejudiced, amazingly visual, authoritative and friendly. "

Poet Dylan Thomas in a letter from Italy to John Arlott, June 11 1947

CONTENTS

THE VOICE OF CRICKET

FOR SO many years John Arlott was known as the voice of cricket – but you didn't have to be a lover of the game to appreciate his greatness.

Arlott seized the listener's attention at once with his distinctive Hampshire accent, a peerless genius for coining a memorable phrase and, above all else, with his humanity. So wide was his following beyond the boundaries of cricket, it was said that the audience for *Test Match Special* increased when rain stopped play. Thousands would tune in simply to hear Arlott describe the covers being wheeled on and off.

It is as a describer of cricket that Arlott is best known – and rightly so. For three decades he was the doyen of cricket commentators, and the word-pictures he painted of Test matches came to be admired all across the world. But Arlott's enthusiasms stretched far beyond the confines of cricket grounds. He was a young beat copper in Southampton, a poetry producer for the BBC and a highly-regarded minor poet in his own right; he wrote over 90 books, taking in cricket histories, poetry volumes, biographies, the theatre, cheese, football, photography, snuff, Champagne, the wines of Burgundy, and other subjects beside. In addition he found time to be a devoted dad, an exceptionally prolific journalist and a tireless campaigner for good causes close to his heart.

He also had a rare gift for friendship and hospitality: guests sitting down for lunch chez Arlott could expect still to be seated at midnight, as their host provided a limitless supply of reinforcements from his cellar – the compiling of which was a life's work in its own right. Above all, Arlott was a deeply moral man. He abhorred violence or injustice of any kind, and the Liberal politics and respect for his fellow man he had learned in boyhood formed his character and gave him his ethical compass. It was no accident that while the cricketing establishment was equivocal in its opposition to apartheid, Arlott courageously spoke out against sporting links with South Africa when the cause was far from fashionable.

It was not all bats, books and booze for Arlott. There was tragedy along the way, and on occasions the sunshine only served to make the shadows darker. But through it all he retained the engaging humanity that was obvious to anybody who heard him speak. The public recognised in Arlott a sincerity impossible to fake. In this country we do not readily invite strangers into our home, but Arlott – one of the great Englishmen of the 20th Century – was always welcome. Even for people who would not know silly mid-off from a sideboard.

Alex Murphy

THE NATURE OF CRICKET

Picture: John Arlott at the BBC in 1955.

FAST BOWLING

" There is no more savagely moving sight than to be part of a crowd watching a fast bowler – better still a pair of fast bowlers – knocking down wickets. When the pitch is fast or green, preferably both, and batsmen are being tumbled out, the temper of the crowd becomes almost primitive. Each time a wicket falls, the killer howl goes up. "

LONELINESS

❝ Cricket is a game of the most terrifying stresses with more luck about it than any other game I know. They call it a team game but it is in fact the loneliest game I know. ❞

HUMAN NATURE

" Cricket, like the novel, is great when it presents men in the round, when it shows the salty quality of human nature. "

DEPTH

" Most games are skin deep but cricket goes to the bone. "

" This is a game of such resource and depth that the national character and the people's character is reflected in it. "

LIFE

" Say that cricket has nothing to do with politics and you say that cricket has nothing to do with life. "

MONEY

" Money can't buy you happiness but it allows you to be miserable in comfort. **"**

THE WEATHER

" The President of the Immortals – or the lesser person with arbitrary control over the English weather – played Hampshire like a small fish on a strong line to the last moment. "

Worcestershire win the 1974 County Championship when Hampshire's match against Yorkshire is abandoned without a ball being bowled.

FAILURE

❝ My word I know what the problems are.
I've failed at everything. **❞**

**Asked if his commentaries might have been helped if
he had played first-class cricket.**

MYTHOLOGY

" If you're a little boy following Hampshire or a Yorkshire boy, a Leicestershire boy, a Kent boy, the cricket of that county creates in your mind a mythology of that particular county and once you've done that, it stays with you always. "

EDUCATION

" Cricket is not a game for the untutored. **"**

PROFOUND

" It is a game of the greatest profundity, of incredible profundity, and (unless you are going to include chess) the deepest game in the world. **"**

MANN TO MANN

" It is I suppose a case of Mann's inhumanity to Mann. "
South African spinner Tufty Mann ties Middlesex batsman George Mann in knots.

THE LIBERAL

Picture: Arlott canvassing in Epping where he stood as the Liberal candidate in the 1959 General Election.

LIBERALISM

" Mr Gladstone, who was at one time a Conservative and who joined the Liberal Party, put it quite clearly – and I think it's the best exposition of the difference I know. Gladstone cherished conservatism, there's no doubt – particularly with a small 'c' – he wanted to save many of the things that were good, and rich, and traditional. Yet he said: 'My sympathies are with the Conservatives, but my opinions are with the Liberals'. "

RADICALISM

" The basis of the British Liberal Party is the radical movement, which is fundamentally an anti-Conservative movement. "

LORD'S

“ The rejection of D'Oliveira has made a breach in the walls of Lord's Cricket Ground through which international opinion has surged in to make, for the first time, an impact on the self-perpetuating committee of a private club. ”

Writing in *The Guardian* about the international outrage at the omission of Basil D'Oliveira from the 1968 MCC team for South Africa.

LIBERTY

" On either side he (a Liberal) will abhor the loss of freedom and liberty; he must at all costs be a liberal person – that is, have a belief in the individual, be prepared to be generous on both sides; he must be prepared to grant liberty and freedom, which is his creed. He isn't a Conservative and he isn't a socialist – he's a Liberal. **"**

BELIEF

" I am in politics because I believe in Liberalism and for that reason only.
I am a completely unrepentant Liberal. "

ELECTIONS

“ Election campaigns are a dizzy, almost giddy life of absolute high pressure with your mind set on only one thing and it did, I found, as nothing else has ever done, obliterate everything else. **”**

Arlott stood as a Liberal candidate for the Epping constituency in two General Elections; 1955 and 1959.

ANGER

" What I've believed in was being violated by the government of this country. I still feel angry now as I did then, now I suspect this anger is shared."

On his adoption as Liberal candidate.

LEADERSHIP

" I sometimes wake in the night with my hair almost standing on end...
I couldn't have done it. I wouldn't have made a party leader, any more
than I could hire or fire. I would never have made a party leader.**"**

On the suggestion that he could have become Liberal leader.

APARTHEID

" There is a time in the growth of some political beliefs when they so offend against common morals that they are recognisable as evil and obnoxious to right-thinking people. I cannot believe that any gentleman on the other side of the house would happily have played a round of golf with Hitler or Goering, nor I trust do any of them want to make up a football match with the people who directed or carried out the suppression of the Hungarian Revolution or who battered down the rise of thought in Dubcek's Czechoslovakia. "

Arlott backs sporting sanctions in a Parliamentary debate on cricketing links with South Africa.

D'OLIVEIRA

❝ It is not an earth-shaking job but I don't think you will find a better one and I do recommend you to accept it. ❞

Letter to Basil D'Oliveira after helping him get a post as League Professional at the Middleton Club in the Central Lancashire League.

CRICKETERS AND CHARACTERS

Picture: Home Secretary Willie Whitelaw presents Arlott with the PYE Radio Sports Personality of the Year Award in 1980. Terry Wogan was Radio Presenter of the Year.

SIR JACK HOBBS

" Sir Jack Hobbs, the man who made batting seem easy.
Who developed the craft more nearly than anyone else to the point
of perfection. Invested it with such ease, subtlety, and invention,
that in his hands it could seem an art. "

" Jack Hobbs was the best man I ever knew in my life.
I would say this even if he never made a run. There was something
incredibly Christ-like about Jack, there really was. "

LEN HUTTON

" You never saw Len play a violent shot nor one that contradicted the flow of the game. **"**

CB FRY

" He had the features of a Greek god, an aquiline nose, an imperious look, wavy hair, impeccable manners, wide shoulders, superbly shaped body and a sense of humour and dignity that never failed him. **"**

FRED TRUEMAN

" He was a cocked trigger, left arm pointed high, head steady, eyes glaring at the batsman as that great stride widened, the arm slashed down and as the ball was fired down the pitch, the body was thrown after it, the right toe raking the ground closely behind the wicket as he swept on. "

From *Fred: Portrait Of A Fast Bowler*.

" Fred Trueman the man has often been tactless, haphazard, crude, a creature of impulse. "

JIM LAKER

66 I think there is no doubt that Jim Laker is the greatest off-spinner that ever was. **99**

66 They said that down at the non-striker's end you heard the ball buzz as it left his fingers. **99**

VIV RICHARDS

" Batting for Vivian Richards is a matter of strokes, more strokes,
and even more strokes. "

" About this time someone described him as a young bull. There was
in his approach that majestic rhythm that emerges as a surprise in the
Spanish fighting bull. It steps out of the toril, stands hesitant, cumbersome,
then suddenly sights the peón from the cuadrilla, pulls itself up and sets
off towards him in a mounting glory of rhythm, power and majesty. "

HERBERT STRUDWICK

" He paid for his devotion with some savage injuries. To his death he had a thumb-sized hole in his ribs from being hit by an edged fast ball, but he played in the next match. The flimsy wicket-keeping glove of his early years gave little protection; and his fingers fractured so often that they were misshapen and knotted as oak twigs. **"**

From an obituary printed in *The Guardian* in 1970. Strudwick was one of the great wicket-keepers. He played for Surrey from 1898 to 1927 and was the county's scorer and wicket-keeping coach until 1960.

DICKIE BIRD

" Dickie Bird standing behind the stumps at the bowler's end looking for all the world like a pantomime goose."

" Not so much examining the pitch as pecking at it."
On Dickie Bird inspecting the wicket.

DON BRADMAN

" Bradman, bowled Hollies, nought. And – what do you say under those circumstances? I wonder if you see a ball very clearly in your last Test in England on a ground where you've played some of the biggest cricket of your life, and when the opposing team have just stood round you and given three cheers and the crowd has clapped you all the way to the wicket. I wonder if you really see the ball at all. "

**Commentary on Don Bradman's last innings in a Test in England,
The Oval, August 14 1948.**

" I do not think cricket is under Bradman's skin,
but I believe that it is under his skull. "

BRIAN JOHNSTON

" A man with a music-hall imagination. **"**

GEOFFREY BOYCOTT

" As Boycott sighted his ambition close ahead he began to walk into the bowling, pushing it away with a bat which seemed all unmissable middle. Urged on by the crowd he scored steadily in singles and twos until the final four, a stroke of utter command. Long after play ended a crowd before the pavilion chanted, called for, and celebrated him. "

Arlott's description in *The Guardian* of Geoff Boycott scoring his 100th hundred – against Australia at Headingley in 1977.

" Even those who like him least are compelled to respect his utter dedication. "

GARRY SOBERS

"When he walked out to bat, six feet tall, lithe but with adequately wide shoulders, he moved with long strides which, even when he was hurrying, had an air of laziness, the hip joints rippling like those of a giant cat."

BILL EDRICH

" One of these days I am convinced Edrich will burst on the way
to the crease. As it is he merely explodes when he gets there.
It's an amazing action. He leans forward, goes up on tiptoes and
gradually with a heel-swung gallop he flings that one down at
Bradman and it moved in the air… It's quite fast, it's not by any means
as fast as Lindwall and it's a slingy action and it's completely out of the
normal traditions of fast bowling but it certainly propels a ball very fast
from one set of wickets in the general direction of the other. "

Commentary, England v Australia, Fourth test, Headingley, 1947.

AUSTRALIANS

" They are not the world's greatest losers. Nobody gets so bitter as Australians.**"**

THE LORD'S STREAKER

" Not very shapely... and it's masculine. He's now being marched in a final exhibition past at least eight thousand people in the Mound Stand, some of whom, perhaps, have never seen anything quite like this before. "

A streaker invades the field at Lord's, Second Test v Australia, 1974.

BILL ATHEY

" Umpire Bill Athey, the solitary dissident. **"**

ERNIE KNIGHTS

" He was profoundly, though never ostentatiously, wise in matters of soil, weather, rolling, raking, cutting above all in making grass grow hardily. "

The Guardian obituary for Hampshire's groundsman in 1979.

CLIVE LLOYD

" Lloyd hits him away over mid-wicket for four,
a stroke of a man knocking a thistle-top off with a walking stick. "

DENNIS LILLEE

" Beginning to show a bit of a bald patch –
lightly tonsured you might say. "

On Dennis Lillee's hairline.

JACK BOND

" Asif stepped out and drove high through a gap at mid-off only for Bond, shedding half his 39 years, to leap up wide to his right and take the catch one-handed at full stretch before falling, holding it exultantly high. "

Jack Bond's catch at extra cover wins the 1971 Gillette Cup for Lancashire.

ABDUL KARDAR

“ Kardar seems at the moment to have about four fieldsmen and seven missionaries, you know, as they used to say in Victorian days, sent into distant fields. They're still in Trent Bridge but only just. **”**

PHILIP MEAD

66 At the fall of Hampshire's second wicket he would emerge from the pavilion with a peculiar rolling gait, his sloping shoulders, wide hips and heavy, bowed legs giving him the bottom-heavy appearance of those lead-based, won't-fall-down dolls of our childhood. 99

66 Philip Mead only ever picked up his bat to score runs – business runs. 99

Mead was the Hampshire batsman who scored the most first-class runs for one team in the history of cricket – 48,892 between 1905 and 1936.

RAY ILLINGWORTH

" And Ray Illingworth is relieving himself in front of the pavilion. **"**
Captain Ray Illingworth relieves himself of bowling duties.

BILL FRINDALL

" Bill Frindall has done a bit of mental arithmetic with a calculator. "

MIKE BREARLEY

" He brought to captaincy a dimension which people had not hitherto perceived. "

DEREK RANDALL

❝ There was a brief, joyous interlude of Randall making the stroke of a happy cricketer, with a full, generous swing of the bat. For almost half an hour he made the method men seem too sad.❞

From *The Guardian* match report on the Headingley Test against Australia in 1977.

ENTHUSIASMS AND OBSERVATIONS

Picture: By 1959 Arlott was a leading radio commentator and sports journalist.

BURGUNDY

" If a local football team calls itself Basingstoke Arsenal, it will not win the FA Cup because of the name 'Arsenal'. By roughly the same token, a wine which calls itself Australian 'Burgundy' is not in fact Burgundy at all. It may be a very pleasant drink but it is not Burgundy because it does not come from Burgundy. Therefore for the first trial, it is wiser to buy the French original. "

VOICES

❝ The records I have chosen would bring me the voices of home, the songs of the people of the countryside – my people – songs that originated in the rural nursery or the village pub... and the glorious sweeps of trained and rare operatic voices… and the world-weary voices of the West End bandstand.**❞**

To Roy Plomley on *Desert Island Discs*, 1953.

CHOIRS

" If I were asked to choose just one record to epitomise England, it would be the choir of King's College Chapel, Cambridge, singing *In Dulce Jubilo*. To attend evensong in that chapel on a winter's afternoon when the candles are lighted seems to me an almost unbearable glory for the eyes, the ears and the mind. "

Desert Island Discs

BOOKS

" Think of the happy years I could spend, browsing and arranging, of the treasures I might find – rare first editions and association copies. **"**

On his desert island luxury – a second-hand bookshop.

HAMBLEDON

" A hundred and seventy years ago there were giants in Hampshire. If you walk up the road from Hambledon, past Park Gate, towards Clanfield, you will come to an old red-brick and tile inn, bleaching in the sun; across the road from it there is a great bare Hampshire down. Don't walk by without looking at it; it's the home of the giants – the old inn is the Bat and Ball and the down is Broadhalfpenny Down, the ground of Hambledon Cricket Club, the greatest single club in the history of cricket. "

VILLAGERS

" Villagers do not think village cricket is funny.**"**

PLEASURE

" Drinking is pleasurable, betting is pleasurable, smoking is pleasurable and, if I dare say it on the air of the British Broadcasting Corporation, sex is pleasurable and exciting. "

In a radio debate about abstinence with Methodist preacher, Dr Donald Soper.

UMPIRES

❝ It occurs to me, Trevor, that it is rather suitable for umpires to look like dentists since one of their duties is to draw stumps. **❞**

HARDY

" I had just got to the point where Jude and Sue open the closet door and find the bodies of the three children hanging there. I dropped the book and dashed down six flights of stairs to find anybody who could speak English – I was so frightened. "

On reading *Jude The Obscure* in an Austrian hotel room.

BRANDY

" For medicinal purposes only. I shan't enjoy it.**"**
On his retirement post-breakfast tipple.

COMMENTARY

" I talk about what I see. A lot of commentators tend to talk about what they are thinking rather than what they are watching. **"**

AUSTRALIA

" It is a dull country: the people much of a hearty sameness and none of the things that interest me available in more than driblets – virtually no second-hand bookshops, barebones of worthwhile architecture, no pottery, no glass, no pictures. "

ARSENAL

" Arsenal are something of a test case of rough play. Derek Tapscott is the most impassioned tumbler in the business: his falling is so dramatic that if he were not such a successful goal-poacher he could make a fortune on the stage as the victim in murder plays. "

LAWN MOWERS

❝ It's a lot less bovver than a hover. **❞**
For Qualcast lawn mowers.

REWARDS

" To get paid £10,000 for standing in a field in Cambridgeshire, I'd say virtually anything. "

Arlott reflects on taking the Qualcast shilling.

BISCUITS

" When summers were just a bit longer and hotter, when we still had pounds, shillings and pence – and guineas – and you listened to wirelesses not transistors and you travelled to Devon on the Great Western Railway. If you can remember any of these things, these Huntley and Palmer biscuits will take you back a bit. I'd almost forgotten a biscuit could taste as good as this. "

METAPHORS AND MUSINGS

Picture: Arlott in the commentary box for his final *Test Match Special* – the Centenary Test at Lord's between England and Australia, September 2, 1980.

PALELY LOITERING

" He passes Boycott, who's got his helmet underneath his arm, like a knight at arms alone and palely loitering. "

WASPS' NEST

" Like an old lady poking with her umbrella at a wasps' nest. "
On Australian tail-ender Ernie Toshack's batting.

STEALING JAM

" Butcher drops his head, both hands behind his back, and looks sheepishly down the wicket like a small boy stealing jam."

Arlott paints a vivid picture of Surrey and England batsman Alan Butcher.

SCHOOLBOY

" Like a cross between a Viking and an irresponsible schoolboy. **"**
On Australian all-rounder Keith Miller.

SHIRE HORSE

“ Botham runs in like a shire horse cresting the breeze. ”

LORD LONGFORD

" Van der Bijl is coming on to bowl looking like a taller, healthier, stronger version of Lord Longford. But not nearly so tolerant. "

On Middlesex's South African fast bowler Vincent Van der Bijl.

CASSEROLE

" What I really want to know, Bill, is if England bowl their overs at the same rate as Australia did, and Brearley and Boycott survive the opening spell, and the number of no-balls is limited to ten in the innings, and assuming my car does 33.8 miles per gallon and my home is 67.3 miles from the ground, what time does my wife have to put the casserole in? "

PRETTY WAITRESS

" He approaches the wicket like Groucho Marx chasing a pretty waitress. "

On Pakistani fast-bowler Asif Masood's distinctive action.

WEARY STORK

❝ The umpire signals a bye with the air of a weary stork. **❞**

LAST WORD

" Bright again going round the wicket to the right-handed Boycott, and Boycott pushes this away between silly point and slip, picked up by Mallett at short third man, that's the end of the over, it's 69 for two, nine runs off the over, 28 Boycott, 15 Gower, 69 for two and after Trevor Bailey it'll be Christopher Martin-Jenkins. "

Last-ever words of Test Match commentary, England v Australia, Lord's, 1980.

EPITAPH

" So clear you see these timeless things
That, like a bird, the vision sings. "

**From Arlott's poem honouring Andrew Young, inscribed on Arlott's
gravestone on Alderney.**

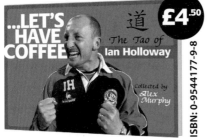
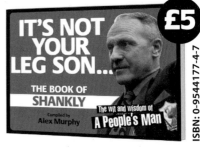